PRAYERS of the DESERT

INTRODUCTION
Page 3

THE RULE OF SAINT PACHOMIUS
Page 8

THE OFFICE OF THE TWELVE PSALMS
Page 14

EVAGRIUS PONTICUS: 153 TEXTS ON PRAYER
Page 51

Copyright © 2020, 2024 Saint Ignatius Orthodox Press
www.ignatius.cc

In partnership with Legacy Icons
www.legacyicons.com

All Rights Reserved

Adapted from the *Anthologion,* Saint Ignatius Orthodox Press
Edited by Reader John Dykstra
Project Oversight by David DeJonge

ISBN 979-8-9865301-6-1

Third Printing, 2024
Printed in China

INTRODUCTION

Dating from the early centuries of undivided Christianity (ca. 3rd–4th centuries), the founders of monasticism in deserts of Egypt have left us tremendous treasures that speak to us across the centuries. These writings are a testament to the Spirit of God which inspired them, and their words have much to offer us today.

THE RULE OF SAINT PACHOMIUS

Saint Pachomius the Great (ca. 290–348) was an early Christian monk, and is considered the founder of *cenobitic* monasticism—a form monasticism that stresses the importance of sharing a common community life within a monastery. (In contrast to *eremetic* monasticism, in which monks live a mostly solitary life.) He established several monasteries in the deserts of Upper Egypt.[1]

Abba Pachomius was the first monastic leader to establish a formal rule of life for his monasteries.

---

[1] *In the regions surrounding modern-day Qena, Egypt.*

This included his prayer rule, which he expected his monks to pray each day. According to tradition, this short prayer rule was revealed to him by an angel. Abba Pachomius himself maintained it faithfully throughout his life, reciting it at every hour of the day and night. As many of his monks were illiterate, the prayer rule is simple and easy to memorize, having the Jesus Prayer at its heart, together with other common prayers. It is believed that Saint Pachomius started the practice of using a prayer rope with his prayer rule, as an aid to keeping track of recitations without needing to focus on counting.

In our modern world, literacy is high, and many different prayer books are available. Nevertheless, it is profitable to know a simple prayer rule like Saint Pachomius', because it can be easily recalled from memory and prayerfully recited while commuting, during work, in any place or at any time of day.

THE OFFICE OF THE TWELVE PSALMS

Like the Rule of Saint Pachomius, this prayer service developed out of the early Christian monastic tradition, in which the entire Book of Psalms was read in a structured fashion every single day.

Over time, other hymns and prayers were added to these daily Psalm readings to enrich the prayers. At the same time, the simpler Twelve Psalms service developed as a substitute for the daily services of Matins, Vespers, and the Hours.

The Twelve Psalms were prayed especially in small monasteries, or *sketes*, in which the many books required for full liturgical worship services were not available, or in which the monks did not have the skill or ability to perform them. (Note that the Twelve Psalms were never meant to replace a person's normal personal prayer rule, but to compliment it, in the same way that church services compliment our personal prayers.)

In today's world, we see how easily our access to the Church's divine services can be cut off, whether due to pandemic, civil unrest, or violence. God forbid, but we cannot take for granted that we will always be able to attend Church when we desire it. To remain in the life of the Church, we must take on the responsibility of prayer ourselves. In such circumstances, we can look to our spiritual ancestors in the ancient deserts, who became like angels in their simple lives of constant prayer.

Whether prevented from attending Church due to illness, travel, or other circumstances, or if one simply desires to observe the Church's cycle of prayer in an uncomplicated way, the time-tested prayers of the Twelve Psalms have led countless souls on the road to salvation.

THE 153 TEXTS ON PRAYER

These texts were written by Evagrius Ponticus, known as "the Solitary" (ca. 345–399). He was born into a Christian family in Heraclea Pontica.[2] Evagrius was educated by the best minds of his day, studying under the great fathers of the Church, Saints Basil the Great and Gregory of Nazianzus.

Evagrius rose through the minor orders of the clergy—being tonsured a reader, then being elevated to subdeacon. He was later promoted to the major order of deacon, and then to archdeacon. At the age of 36, he was present at the Second Ecumenical Council in Constantinople in the year 381.

Even as a member of the clergy, Evagrius lived a very worldly life, full of vanity and sinful relationships with married women. By God's mercy, he recieved a terrifying vision that shook him to his core,

[2]*Modern-day Karadeniz Ereğli, Türkiye.*

and he was warned by an angel to flee to Jerusalem.

He attached himself to a monastery near the Holy City, but even there he could not shake off his pride and vanity. After being struck with a serious illness, he finally confessed his sins and entered the monastic life in repentance. He spent a few years in Jerusalem, and then departed to the desert monasteries of Upper Egypt,[3] where he studied the spiritual life under the guidance of the famous Desert Fathers.

Under the guidance of Saints Macarius the Great and Macarius of Alexandria, Evagrius spent fourteen years in extreme asceticism and repentance for his sins. He reposed in the year 399, leaving behind stories of his life written by others who knew him, as well as his own writings, which have left a lasting impression on Eastern Christian spirituality.

Among his wise words that have passed down to us are his *153 Texts On Prayer*, which are found in the collection of ascetic writings known as the *Philokalia*. While his *153 Texts* were written to an unnamed monk, these bite-sized pieces of deep spiritual wisdom based on his experiences of repentance are edifying to all those who are seeking to truly pray and live a life of holiness. ✟

---

[3]*In the regions surrounding modern-day Luxor, Egypt.*

THE RULE OF SAINT PACHOMIUS

Through the prayers of our holy fathers, O Lord Jesus Christ, our God, have mercy on us. Amen.

Glory to you, our God, glory to you.

O Heavenly King, Comforter, Spirit of Truth, present everywhere, filling all things, Treasury of blessings and Giver of life, come and dwell in us, cleanse us from every stain, and, O Good One, save our souls.

THE TRISAGION PRAYERS

Holy God, Holy Mighty, Holy Immortal, have mercy on us. (3)

Glory to the Father and to the Son and to the Holy Spirit, both now and forever, and to the ages of ages. Amen.

All-Holy Trinity, have mercy on us. Lord, forgive our sins. Master, pardon our iniquities. Holy One, visit and heal our infirmities for your Name's sake.

Lord, have mercy. (3)

Glory to the Father and to the Son and to the Holy Spirit, both now and forever, and to the ages of ages. Amen.

Our Father in heaven, may your Name be hallowed, your Kingdom come, your will be done on earth as in heaven. Give us today our daily bread. And forgive us our debts, as we forgive our debtors. And do not lead us into temptation, but deliver us from the evil one.

Through the prayers of our holy fathers, O Lord Jesus Christ, our God, have mercy on us. Amen.

Lord, have mercy. (12)

Glory to the Father and to the Son and to the Holy Spirit, both now and forever, and to the ages of ages. Amen.

Come, let us worship and fall down before the King, our God.
Come, let us worship and fall down before Christ, the King, our God.
Come, let us worship and fall down before him, Christ the King and our God.

PSALM 50

Have mercy on me, O God, in your great mercy; according to the fullness of your compassion, blot out my offense.

Wash me thoroughly from my wickedness, and cleanse me from my sin.

For I acknowledge my wickedness, and my sin is ever before me.

Against you only have I sinned and done what is evil in your sight,

That you may be justified in your words, and prevail when you are judged.

For behold, in wickedness I was conceived, and in sin my mother bore me.

For behold, you have loved truth: you have shown me the hidden and secret things of your wisdom.

You will sprinkle me with hyssop, and I shall be cleansed; you will wash me, and I shall be made whiter than snow.

You will make me hear of joy and gladness; the bones which have been humbled will rejoice.

Turn away your face from my sins, and blot out all my iniquities.

Create a clean heart in me, O God, and renew a right Spirit within me.

Do not cast me out from your presence, and do not take your Holy Spirit from me.

Give me back the joy of your salvation, and establish me with a sovereign Spirit.

I will teach transgressors your ways, and sinners will turn to you again.

O God, the God of my salvation, deliver me from bloodshed, and my tongue will rejoice at your righteousness.

O Lord, you will open my lips, and my mouth will declare your praise.

For if you had wanted a sacrifice, I would have given it; you will not take pleasure in burnt offerings.

A sacrifice to God is a broken spirit; a broken and a humbled heart God will not despise.

Do good to Zion, O Lord, in your good pleasure, and let the walls of Jerusalem be rebuilt.

Then you will be well-pleased with a sacrifice of righteousness, oblation and whole burnt offerings.

Then they will offer calves upon your altar.

THE CREED

I believe in one God, Father Almighty, Maker of heaven and earth, of all things visible and invisible.

And in one Lord Jesus Christ, the Only-begotten Son of God, begotten from the Father before all ages. Light from Light, true God from true God, begotten, not made, consubstantial with the Father; through him all things were made; for our sake and for our salvation came down from heaven, and was incarnate from the Holy Spirit and the Virgin Mary and became man; he was crucified also for us under Pontius Pilate, and suffered and was buried; he rose again on the third day, in accordance with the Scriptures, and ascended into heaven and is seated at the right hand of the Father; he is coming again in glory to judge the living and the dead; and his Kingdom will have no end.

And in the Holy Spirit, the Lord, the Giver of life, who proceeds from the Father, who together with the Father and the Son is worshiped and together glorified; who spoke through the Prophets. In one, Holy, Catholic and Apostolic Church; I confess one

Baptism for the forgiveness of sins. I await the Resurrection of the dead and the life of the age to come. Amen.

THE JESUS PRAYER

O LORD, Jesus Christ, Son of God, have mercy on me, a sinner. (100)

THE DISMISSAL

It is truly right to call you blessed, who gave birth to God, ever-blessed and most pure and the Mother of our God. Greater in honor than the Cherubim and beyond compare more glorious than the Seraphim, without corruption you gave birth to God the Word; truly the Mother of God, we magnify you.

Glory to the Father and to the Son and to the Holy Spirit, both now and forever, and to the ages of ages. Amen.

Lord, have mercy. (3)

Through the prayers of our holy fathers, O Lord Jesus Christ, our God, have mercy on us. Amen. ✠

THE OFFICE OF THE TWELVE PSALMS

Through the prayers of our holy fathers, O Lord Jesus Christ, our God, have mercy on us. Amen.

Glory to you, our God, glory to you.

O Heavenly King, Comforter, Spirit of Truth, present everywhere, filling all things, Treasury of blessings and Giver of life, come and dwell in us, cleanse us from every stain, and, O Good One, save our souls.

THE TRISAGION PRAYERS

Holy God, Holy Mighty, Holy Immortal, have mercy on us. (3)

Glory to the Father and to the Son and to the Holy Spirit, both now and forever, and to the ages of ages. Amen.

All-Holy Trinity, have mercy on us. Lord, forgive our sins. Master, pardon our iniquities. Holy One, visit and heal our infirmities for your Name's sake.

Lord, have mercy. (3)

Glory to the Father and to the Son and to the Holy Spirit, both now and forever, and to the ages of ages. Amen.

Our Father in heaven, may your Name be hallowed, your Kingdom come, your will be done on earth as in heaven. Give us today our daily bread. And forgive us our debts, as we forgive our debtors. And do not lead us into temptation, but deliver us from the evil one.

Through the prayers of our holy fathers, O Lord Jesus Christ, our God, have mercy on us. Amen.

Lord, have mercy. (12)

Glory to the Father and to the Son and to the Holy Spirit, both now and forever, and to the ages of ages. Amen.

Now continue with the appointed Stases (sections) according to the chart on the next page.

After saying the usual beginning prayers (pages 12–13), continue with the Stases appointed for the present service:

OUTSIDE LENT		
FOR SERVICE	STASES	PAGES
Matins	I, II, III, IV	15–47
The Hours	I, II	15–29
Vespers	III, IV	29–47
Compline	III, IV	29–47

DURING LENT & FASTING SEASONS		
FOR SERVICE	STASES	PAGES
Matins	I, II, III, IV	15–47
The Hours	I, II, III	15–37
Vespers	I, II, III	15–37
Compline	IV	37–47

And finally, after completing the appointed Stases, conclude at all times with the Dismissal (pages 47–48).

FIRST STASIS

Come, let us worship and fall down before the King, our God.

Come, let us worship and fall down before Christ, the King, our God.

Come, let us worship and fall down before him, Christ the King and our God.

PSALM 26

The Lord is my enlightenment and my Savior; whom shall I fear? The Lord is the defender of my life; of whom shall I be afraid?

When evildoers came against me to eat up my flesh, my persecutors and my enemies, they fainted and fell.

Though an army should array itself against me, my heart shall not fear; though war should rise up against me, in this I hope.

I have asked one thing of the Lord, this will I earnestly seek: That I should dwell in the house of the Lord all the days of my life, that I should behold the fair beauty of the Lord, and survey his temple.

For in the day of my afflictions he hid me in his tabernacle, he sheltered me in the secret of his tabernacle, he set me up on a rock.

And now, behold, he has lifted up my head over my enemies.

I went around and offered in his tabernacle the sacrifice of rejoicing; I will sing, I will sing psalms to the Lord.

O Lord, hear my voice which I have raised; have mercy on me, and hear me.

My heart said to you: I have diligently sought your face. Your face, O Lord, will I seek.

Do not turn your face away from me; do not turn away from your servant in anger.

Be my helper; do not forsake me, and do not overlook me, O God my Savior.

My father and my mother have forsaken me, but the Lord has taken me to himself.

Teach me your way, O Lord, and guide me in a right path because of my enemies.

Do not hand me over to the desire of those who torment me, for unjust witnesses have risen up against me, and injustice has lied within herself.

I believe that I will see the good things of the Lord in the land of the living.

Wait on the Lord; be of good courage, and let your heart be strengthened, and wait on the Lord.

PSALM 31

Blessed are they whose iniquities are forgiven, and whose sins are covered.

Blessed is the one whom the Lord will by no means charge with sin, and in whose mouth there is no guile.

Because I kept silent, my bones grew old from my crying out all day long.

For night and day your hand was heavy upon me, I was turned to wretchedness by a thorn stuck fast in me.

I acknowledged my sin, and did not hide my iniquity. I said: Against myself I will admit my iniquity to the Lord. And you forgave the ungodliness of my heart.

For this, every holy one shall pray to you at a fitting moment. Except in a flood of many waters they will not come near him.

For you are my refuge from the affliction which surrounds me; O my Joy, deliver me from those who have surrounded me.

I will make you understand and guide you in the way in which you should go; I will fix my eyes upon you.

Do not become like horse and mule, who have no understanding; with bit and bridle you must constrain their cheeks so that they do not come near you.

Many are the scourges of the sinner, but mercy will surround the one who hopes in the Lord.

Rejoice in the Lord, and be glad, you righteous, and boast, all you upright in heart.

PSALM 56

Have mercy on me, O God, have mercy on me; for my soul has trusted in you.

And in the shadow of your wings will I hope, until iniquity pass by.

I will cry to God Most High, the God who has done good things for me.

He sent from heaven and saved me; he gave to reproach those who trampled on me.

God has sent forth his mercy and his truth, and he has delivered my soul from the midst of lions' cubs; I lay down to sleep, but I am troubled.

THE OFFICE OF THE TWELVE PSALMS: STASIS I

As for the sons of men, their teeth are weapons and arrows, and their tongue a sharp sword.

Be exalted, O God, above the heavens, and your glory above all the earth.

They have set a trap for my feet, and have bowed down my soul.

They have dug a pit before me and have fallen into it themselves.

My heart is ready, O God, my heart is ready; I will sing, I will sing psalms.

Rise up, O my glory; rise up, O psaltery and harp; I will rise up early at dawn.

I will confess you, O Lord, among the nations; I will sing to you among the nations.

For your mercy has been magnified even to the heavens, and your truth to the clouds.

Be exalted, O God, above the heavens, and your glory above all the earth.

THE TRISAGION PRAYERS

Holy God, Holy Mighty, Holy Immortal, have mercy on us. (3)

Glory to the Father and to the Son and to the Holy Spirit, both now and forever, and to the ages of ages. Amen.

All-Holy Trinity, have mercy on us. Lord, forgive our sins. Master, pardon our iniquities. Holy One, visit and heal our infirmities for your Name's sake.

Lord, have mercy. (3)

Glory to the Father and to the Son and to the Holy Spirit, both now and forever, and to the ages of ages. Amen.

Our Father in heaven, may your Name be hallowed, your Kingdom come, your will be done on earth as in heaven. Give us today our daily bread. And forgive us our debts, as we forgive our debtors. And do not lead us into temptation, but deliver us from the evil one.

Through the prayers of our holy fathers, O Lord Jesus Christ, our God, have mercy on us. Amen.

TROPARIA. TONE 1

Hasten to open to me your fatherly embrace; prodigally I have squandered my whole life, turning from your compassion, O Savior, to wealth which cannot be spent; do not now despise my beggared heart; for to you, O Lord, with compunction I cry: I have sinned against you, save me!

Glory to the Father and to the Son and to the Holy Spirit.

WHEN you come to earth with glory, O God, the whole world will tremble. The river of fire will flow from your judgment-seat; the books will be opened, and the secrets will be revealed. Deliver me, then, from that unquenchable fire, and count me worthy to stand at your right hand, O Judge most just.

Both now and forever, and to the ages of ages. Amen.

ALL we who with longing flee for refuge to your goodness know you to be Mother of God, and after childbirth, still truly Virgin; for we sinners have you as protection; in temptations we have you as salvation, the only All-blameless one.

Lord, have mercy. (30)

Glory to the Father and to the Son and to the Holy Spirit, both now and forever, and to the ages of ages. Amen.

SECOND STASIS

Come, let us worship and fall down before the King, our God.

Come, let us worship and fall down before Christ, the King, our God.

Come, let us worship and fall down before him, Christ the King and our God.

PSALM 33

I will bless the Lord continually; his praise shall always be in my mouth.

Let my soul boast of the Lord, the humble will hear it and rejoice.

O magnify the Lord with me; let us exalt his Name together.

For I sought the Lord, and he hearkened to me, and he freed me from all my troubles.

Come to him and be enlightened, and your faces shall not be ashamed.

Here is a poor man who cried, and the Lord heard him, and saved him from all his troubles.

The angel of the Lord will encamp round those who fear him, and deliver them.

O taste and see that the Lord is good; blessed is the man who hopes in him!

O fear the Lord, all you his saints, for those who fear him never lack.

The rich became poor and went hungry, but those who seek the Lord shall lack nothing good.

Come, my children, listen to me; I will teach you the fear of the Lord.

Who is there who wants life, who loves to see good days?

Keep your tongue from evil, and your lips from speaking deceit.

Turn away from evil and do good; seek peace and pursue it.

The eyes of the Lord are on the righteous, and his ears are open to their prayer.

The face of the Lord is against those who do evil, to root out their memory from the earth.

The righteous cried, and the Lord heard them, and freed them from all their troubles.

The Lord is close to those who are broken-hearted, and will save the humble in spirit.

The troubles of the righteous are many, but the Lord will deliver them from them all.

The Lord guards all their bones, not one of them will be broken.

The death of sinners is evil, and those who hate the righteous shall go astray.

The Lord will redeem the souls of his servants, and none who hope in him will go astray.

PSALM 38

I said: I will guard my ways, that I may not sin with my tongue.

I set a guard on my mouth, while the sinner stood in my presence.

I kept silent and was humbled, and held my tongue, even from good words, and my suffering was renewed.

My heart grew hot within me, and in my meditation a fire would burn.

I spoke with my tongue: O Lord, let me know my end, and the number of my days, what it is, that I may know what I lack.

Behold, you have made my days as a hand's breadth, and my existence is as nothing in your sight.

Indeed, every man alive is altogether vanity.

THE OFFICE OF THE TWELVE PSALMS: STASIS II

Surely man passes as a shadow; his turmoil is vanity.

He lays up treasures, but does not know for whom he gathers them.

And now, what is my endurance? Is it not the Lord? My hope is from you.

Deliver me from all my transgressions; you have made me a reproach to fools.

I was silent, and shut my mouth, for you are my Maker.

Remove your scourges from me; I have fainted under the force of your hand.

You rebuke man for sin, and you melt his life away like a spider's web; truly, every man's turmoil is vanity.

Hear my prayer, O Lord, and my supplication; listen to my tears.

Do not be silent, for I am a traveler in the land, and a stranger, as were all my fathers.

Spare me, that I may be refreshed before I depart, and be no more.

PSALM 40

Blessed is the man who considers the poor and needy; in an evil day the Lord will deliver him.

May the Lord guard him, and preserve his life, and bless him on the earth, and not deliver him into the hands of his enemy.

May the Lord help him on the bed of his pain; in his sickness you have restored him.

I said: O Lord, have mercy on me, heal my soul, for I have sinned against you.

My enemies have spoken evil against me: When will he die, and his name perish?

And though he came to visit me, his heart spoke vanity; he gathered iniquity to himself; he went out, and spoke in the same manner.

All my enemies whispered against me; they plotted evil against me.

They spoke a wicked word against me: Surely one who sleeps will not rise up again.

For even the man at peace with me, in whom I trusted, who ate my bread, has lifted up his heel against me.

But you, O Lord, have mercy on me, and raise me up, and I will repay them.

By this I know that you delight in me, because my enemy shall not rejoice over me.

But you helped me because of my innocence, and have established me in your sight forever.

Blessed is the Lord God of Israel, from everlasting to everlasting. So be it, so be it.

THE TRISAGION PRAYERS

Holy God, Holy Mighty, Holy Immortal, have mercy on us. (3)

Glory to the Father and to the Son and to the Holy Spirit, both now and forever, and to the ages of ages. Amen.

All-Holy Trinity, have mercy on us. Lord, forgive our sins. Master, pardon our iniquities. Holy One, visit and heal our infirmities for your Name's sake.

Lord, have mercy. (3)

Glory to the Father and to the Son and to the Holy Spirit, both now and forever, and to the ages of ages. Amen.

Our Father in heaven, may your Name be hallowed, your Kingdom come, your will be done on earth as in heaven. Give us today our daily bread. And forgive us our debts, as we forgive our debtors.

And do not lead us into temptation, but deliver us from the evil one.

Through the prayers of our holy fathers, O Lord Jesus Christ, our God, have mercy on us. Amen.

TROPARIA. TONE 4

Visit my humble soul, O Lord, that has squandered its whole life in sins; receive me as you did the Harlot and save me.

Glory to the Father and to the Son and to the Holy Spirit.

I have wasted my whole life, wretch that I am. O Lord, I cry out like the Prodigal with tearful compunction: O Heavenly Father, I have sinned; cleanse me, and save me! Do not despise me, who have turned away from you, and have become poor because of my fruitless deeds.

Both now and forever, and to the ages of ages. Amen.

Now to God's Mother let us humble sinners run in haste, and in repentance let us fall down before her feet, crying aloud with fervor from the depths of our souls: Sovereign Lady, help us now, have compassion upon us, hasten, for we perish from our many offenses. Let not your servants go empty away; we have you as our only hope.

Lord, have mercy. (30)

Glory to the Father and to the Son and to the Holy Spirit, both now and forever, and to the ages of ages. Amen.

THIRD STASIS

Come, let us worship and fall down before the King, our God.

Come, let us worship and fall down before Christ, the King, our God.

Come, let us worship and fall down before him, Christ the King and our God.

PSALM 69

O GOD, come to my help; O Lord, attend to help me.

Let those who seek my soul be shamed and confounded.

Let those who desire evil for me be turned back and put to shame.

Let those who say to me, Well done, well done! be turned back immediately, ashamed.

Let all who seek you, O God, be glad and rejoice in you.

Let all who love your salvation ever say: The Lord be magnified.

But I am poor and needy; help me, O God.

You are my helper and my deliverer; O Lord, do not delay.

PSALM 70

In you, O Lord, have I hoped; let me not be put to shame forever;

In your righteousness deliver me and rescue me; incline your ear to me and save me.

Be a God to defend me, and a stronghold to save me, for you are my foundation and my refuge.

Deliver me, O my God, from the hand of the sinner, from the hand of the transgressor and wrongdoer.

For you are my endurance, O Lord; O Lord, you are my hope from my youth.

On you have I leaned from the womb; from my mother's womb you are my protector.

Of you is my unending song of praise; I have become as a wonder to many, and you are my strong helper.

Let my mouth be filled with your praise, that I may hymn your glory and your majesty all the day long.

Do not cast me off in my old age; when my strength fails, do not forsake me.

For my enemies have spoken against me, and those who lay in wait for my soul have plotted together, saying: God has forsaken him; persecute him and take him, for there is no one to deliver him.

My God, do not be far from me; my God, attend to help me.

Let those who plot against my soul be ashamed and utterly fail; let those who seek my hurt be clothed with shame and dishonor.

But as for me, I will hope continually, and will praise you more and more.

My mouth will declare your righteousness openly, and your salvation all the day long; for I am not acquainted with the affairs of men.

I will go on in the might of the Lord; O Lord, I will make mention of your righteousness alone.

O my God, you have taught me from my youth, and I will still proclaim your wonders.

Even to old age and advanced years, O my God, do not forsake me,

Until I proclaim your mighty arm to every generation that is to come,

Even your power and your righteousness, O God, up to the highest heavens, even the mighty works that you have done. O God, who is like you?

How great are the afflictions, many and evil, you have shown me! Yet you turned and enlivened me, and brought me up again from the depths of the earth.

You multiplied your righteousness, and turned and comforted me, and brought me again out of the depths of the earth.

Therefore will I confess you, O God, because of your truth, on an instrument of psalmody; I will sing psalms to you on the harp, O Holy One of Israel.

My lips will rejoice when I sing to you, and my soul which you have redeemed.

And my tongue will also meditate on your righteousness all the day long, when they will be ashamed and confounded that seek evils for me.

PSALM 76

I called to the Lord with my voice, with my voice to God, and he heard me.

In the day of my trouble, I sought the Lord with my hands lifted up by night before him, and I was not deceived.

My soul refused to be comforted; I remembered God, and I was glad; I spoke idly, and my soul grew faint.

My eyes were wakeful and kept watch; I was troubled and did not speak.

I considered the days of old, and remembered ancient years, and I meditated.

I pondered in my heart by night, and diligently searched my spirit, saying:

Will the Lord cast me off forever, and will he find favor no more?

Will he cut off his mercy forever, from generation to generation?

Will God forget to have mercy? Or will he shut up his compassions in his wrath?

And I said: Now have I begun; this change is of the right hand of the Most High.

I have remembered the works of the Lord; for I will remember your wonders from the beginning.

And I will meditate on all your works, and I will consider your ways.

O God, your way is in the sanctuary. What God is great as our God? You are God, who alone works wonders.

You have made your power known among the peoples; with your arm you have redeemed your people, the sons of Jacob and Joseph.

The waters saw you, O Lord, the waters saw you and were afraid; and the depths were troubled.

There was a great roaring of waters, the clouds raised a voice.

For your arrows went abroad; the voice of your thunder rolled.

Your lightnings flashed in the world; the earth quaked and trembled.

Your way is in the sea, and your paths in many waters; and your footsteps cannot be known.

You guided your people as sheep by the hand of Moses and Aaron.

THE TRISAGION PRAYERS

Holy God, Holy Mighty, Holy Immortal, have mercy on us. (3)

Glory to the Father and to the Son and to the Holy Spirit, both now and forever, and to the ages of ages. Amen.

All-Holy Trinity, have mercy on us. Lord, forgive our sins. Master, pardon our iniquities. Holy One, visit and heal our infirmities for your Name's sake.

Lord, have mercy. (3)

Glory to the Father and to the Son and to the Holy Spirit, both now and forever, and to the ages of ages. Amen.

Our Father in heaven, may your Name be hallowed, your Kingdom come, your will be done on earth as in heaven. Give us today our daily bread. And forgive us our debts, as we forgive our debtors. And do not lead us into temptation, but deliver us from the evil one.

Through the prayers of our holy fathers, O Lord Jesus Christ, our God, have mercy on us. Amen.

TROPARIA. TONE 4

I THINK of the fearful Day and weep over my filthy deeds. What answer shall I give to the immortal King? And how shall I, the prodigal, have boldness to look upon the Judge? Have mercy upon me, O compassionate Father, Only-begotten Son, and Holy Spirit.

Glory to the Father and to the Son and to the Holy Spirit.

WHEN you shall sit in just judgment, O Merciful, in the valley of tears, in the place you devised, do not make public my secret acts. Do not put me to shame before the Angels, but spare me and have mercy on me, O God.

Both now and forever, and to the ages of ages. Amen.

OPEN the gate of compassion to us, O blessed Mother of God; hoping in you, may we not fail. Through you, may we be delivered from adversities, for you are the salvation of the Christian race.

Lord, have mercy. (30)

Glory to the Father and to the Son and to the Holy Spirit, both now and forever, and to the ages of ages. Amen.

FOURTH STASIS

Come, let us worship and fall down before the King, our God.

Come, let us worship and fall down before Christ, the King, our God.

Come, let us worship and fall down before him, Christ the King and our God.

PSALM 101

O LORD, hear my prayer, and let my cry come to you.

Do not turn your face from me in the day I am in tribulation. Incline your ear to me; in the day I call upon you, be swift to hear me.

For my days have vanished like smoke, and my bones have been burnt up like brushwood.

I have been smitten like grass, and my heart has been dried up, so that I have forgotten to eat my bread.

My bones have stuck to my flesh, from the sound of my groaning.

I have become like a pelican of the desert; like an owl among ruins.

I have kept vigil, and become like a sparrow, alone upon a house-top.

All day my enemies have reviled me, and those who praised me have sworn an oath against me.

I have eaten ashes as my bread, and mixed my drink with weeping.

From the face of your wrath and your anger; for having lifted me up, you have cast me down.

My days have declined like a shadow, and I have been dried up like grass.

But you, O Lord, abide forever, and your memorial to generation and generation.

You will arise and have mercy on Zion, for it is time to have mercy on her, for the time has come.

For your servants have been well-pleased with her stones, and they will have mercy on her dust.

And the nations will fear your Name, O Lord, and all the kings of the earth your glory.

For the Lord will build up Zion, and appear in his glory.

He has looked on the prayer of the humble, and has not despised their supplication.

Let this be written for another generation, and a people that is being created will praise the Lord.

For the Lord has leaned down from his holy height, he has looked from heaven upon the earth.

To hear the groaning of those in fetters, to free the children of the slain.

To announce the Name of the Lord in Zion, and his praise in Jerusalem.

When peoples are gathered together, and kings to serve the Lord.

He answered him in the way of his strength. Tell me the fewness of my days.

Do not lead me away halfway through my days. Your years are for generations of generations.

In the beginning it was you, O Lord, who laid the foundations of the earth, and the heavens are the works of your hands.

They will perish, but you endure; they will all grow old as a garment;

As a mantle you will roll them up, and they will be changed; but you are the same, and your years will not fail.

Your servants' children shall have their dwelling, and their seed shall be guided forever.

THE PRAYER OF MANASSES, KING OF JUDAH

O LORD Almighty, the God of our Fathers, of Abraham and Isaac and Jacob and of their just seed;

Who made the heaven and the earth with all their array; who shackled the sea by the word of your command;

Who shut up the deep and sealed it with your dread and glorious Name;

Before whom all things shudder and tremble in the presence of your power;

For the majesty of your glory cannot be borne, and the wrath of threat to sinners is irresistible,

And the mercy of your promise is measureless and unsearchable.

For you are the Lord Most High, compassionate, long-suffering and full of mercy, and you repent over the evils of mankind.

You, O Lord, according to the multitude of your goodness, have appointed repentance and forgiveness to those who have sinned against you,

And in the multitude of your mercies you have decreed repentance unto salvation for sinners.

You therefore, O Lord God of Powers, did not appoint repentance for the just, for Abraham and Isaac and Jacob, who did not sin against you,

But you have appointed repentance for me, a sinner, because I have sinned above the number of the sand of the sea.

My iniquities have been multiplied, O Lord, my iniquities have been multiplied, and I am not worthy to raise my eyes and to see the height of heaven because of the multitude of my unjust deeds.

I am bowed down by a heavy iron fetter, so that I cannot lift my head, and there is no respite for me;

Because I have provoked your wrath and done what is evil in your sight, not doing your will nor keeping your commands.

And now I bow the knee of my heart, praying for the goodness which is from you:

I have sinned, O Lord, I have sinned, and I recognize my iniquities; but I ask with supplication:

Forgive me, O Lord, forgive me, and do not destroy me with my iniquities,

Do not be wrathful forever; do not lay up evils for me, nor condemn me to the lowest parts of the earth:

For you are God, the God of the penitent, and in me you will show all your goodness;

For you will save me who am unworthy, according to your great mercy, and I will praise you continually all the days of my life.

For all the powers of heaven praise you, and yours is the glory to the ages of ages. Amen.

THE LITTLE DOXOLOGY

Glory to God in the highest, and on earth peace, goodwill among men.

We praise you, we bless you, we worship you, we glorify you, we give you thanks for your great glory.

O Lord, King, God of heaven, Father Almighty: O Lord, Only-begotten Son, Jesus Christ and Holy Spirit.

O Lord God, Lamb of God, Son of the Father, who take away the sin of the world, have mercy on us; you take away the sins of the world.

Receive our prayer, you who sit on the right hand of the Father, and have mercy on us.

THE OFFICE OF THE TWELVE PSALMS: STASIS IV

For you alone are holy, you alone are Lord, O Jesus Christ, to the glory of God the Father. Amen.

Every evening will I bless you, and I will praise your Name forever, and to ages of ages.

O Lord, you have been our refuge from generation to generation.

I said: O Lord, have mercy on me, heal my soul, for I have sinned against you.

O Lord, I have run to you for refuge; teach me to do your will, for you are my God.

For with you is the source of life, and in your light shall we see light.

O continue your mercy toward those who know you.

Grant, O Lord, this night to keep us without sin.

Blessed are you, O Lord, the God of our fathers, and praised and glorified is your Name to the ages. Amen.

May your mercy, O Lord, be upon us, as we have hoped in you.

Blessed are you, O Lord, teach me your statutes.

Blessed are you, O Master, make me understand your statutes.

Blessed are you, O Holy One, enlighten me your statutes.

Your mercy, O Lord, is forever; do not reject the work of your hands.

To you praise is due, to you song is due, to you glory is due: to the Father and to the Son and to the Holy Spirit, both now and forever, and to the ages of ages. Amen.

PRAYER OF SAINT EUSTRATIUS

I MAGNIFY you greatly, O Lord, because you have looked upon my lowliness, and have not hemmed me into the hands of enemies, but have saved my soul from constraints. And now, O Master, let your hand protect me, and your mercy come upon me, for my soul has been troubled and is greatly afflicted at its departure from this wretched and soiled body of mine. May the evil plan of the adversary never confront and obstruct it, because of the many sins committed by me in this life, in knowledge and in ignorance. Be merciful to me, O Master, and never let my soul see the dark and gloomy sight of the evil demons; but may your bright and shining Angels receive it. Give glory to your holy Name, and bring me by your power to your divine judgment-seat. When I am judged, let not the hand of the ruler of this world seize me to cast me, sinner that I am, into the depths of Hades; but stand by me and be for me a Savior and a helper. Have mercy, O Lord, on my soul, stained with the passions of life, and receive it pure through repentance and confession; for you are blessed to the ages of ages. Amen.

THE TRISAGION PRAYERS

Holy God, Holy Mighty, Holy Immortal, have mercy on us. (3)

Glory to the Father and to the Son and to the Holy Spirit, both now and forever, and to the ages of ages. Amen.

All-Holy Trinity, have mercy on us. Lord, forgive our sins. Master, pardon our iniquities. Holy One, visit and heal our infirmities for your Name's sake.

Lord, have mercy. (3)

Glory to the Father and to the Son and to the Holy Spirit, both now and forever, and to the ages of ages. Amen.

Our Father in heaven, may your Name be hallowed, your Kingdom come, your will be done on earth as in heaven. Give us today our daily bread. And forgive us our debts, as we forgive our debtors.

And do not lead us into temptation, but deliver us from the evil one.

Through the prayers of our holy fathers, O Lord Jesus Christ, our God, have mercy on us. Amen.

TROPARIA. TONE 8

With your compassionate eye, O Lord, see my humiliation, for little by little my life is being squandered, and there is no salvation for me from works; therefore, I ask this: with your compassionate eye, O Lord, see my humiliation and save me.

Glory to the Father and to the Son and to the Holy Spirit.

My time has come to an end, and your dread tribunal is ready. My life passes by, and judgment awaits me; my sentence is fiery torment and the unquenchable flame. But grant me a fountain of tears; quench the inferno by your might, for you desire the salvation of all.

Both now and forever, and to the ages of ages. Amen.

You were born for us from a Virgin and endured crucifixion, O loving Lord; by your death you despoiled Death and revealed resurrection as God; do not despise those whom you fashioned with your own hand; show us your compassion, O Merciful; accept the Mother of God who bore you as she intercedes for us, and save, O our Savior, a people in despair.

Lord, have mercy. (30)

Glory to the Father and to the Son and to the Holy Spirit, both now and forever, and to the ages of ages. Amen.

THE DISMISSAL

After completing the appointed Stases, conclude the service as follows:

Greater in honor than the Cherubim and beyond compare more glorious than the Seraphim, without corruption you gave birth to God the Word; truly the Mother of God, we magnify you.

Glory to the Father and to the Son and to the Holy Spirit, both now and forever, and to the ages of ages. Amen.

Lord, have mercy. (3) O Lord, bless.

O Lord Jesus Christ, Son of God, through the prayers of your all-pure and holy Mother; by the power of the precious and life-giving Cross; through the protection of the honored, Bodiless Powers of heaven; by the intercessions of our venerable and God-bearing fathers; of the holy Prophet David; and of all the Saints, have mercy on me and save me, a sinner, for you are good and love mankind.

Through the prayers of our holy fathers, O Lord Jesus Christ, our God, have mercy on us. Amen. ✠

EVAGRIUS PONTICUS THE SOLITARY
153 TEXTS ON PRAYER

PROLOGUE: TO A CERTAIN MONK WHO REQUESTED A WORD

WHEN suffering from the fever of unclean passions, my mind being afflicted with shameful thoughts, I have often been restored to health by your letters, as I was before by the counsel of our great guide and teacher. This is not to be wondered at, since like the blessed Jacob, you have earned a rich inheritance. Through your efforts to win "Rachel," you have been given "Leah,"[a] and now you seek to be given "Rachel" also, since you have labored a further seven years for her sake.

For myself, I cannot deny that although I have labored hard all night, I have caught nothing. Yet at your suggestion I have again let down the nets, and have made a large catch. They are not big "fish,"

[a] Gen. 29:25 [b] John 21:11

but there are a hundred and fifty-three of them.[b] These, as you requested, I am sending you in a "fish-basket" of love, in the form of a hundred and fifty-three texts.

I am delighted to find you so eager for texts on prayer—eager, not simply for those written on paper with ink, but also for those which are fixed in the mind through love and generosity. But since "all things go in pairs, one complimenting the other,"[c] as the wise Jesus [ben Sirach] puts it, please accept the letter and understand its spirit, for every written word presupposes the mind. Where there is no mind, there is no word. The way of prayer is twofold: it comprises practice of the virtues and contemplation. The same applies to numbers: literally they are quantities, but they can also signify qualities. . . .[d]

Do not despise the humble appearance of these texts, for you know how to be content with much or little.[e] You will recall how Christ did not reject the widow's mites,[f] but accepted them as greater than the rich gifts of many others. Showing in this way charity and love towards your true brethren, pray for one who is sick, that he may take up his bed and walk[g] by the grace of Christ. Amen.

[c]*Sirach 42:24* [d]*For brevity we have here omitted his numerological discourse.*
[e]*Phil. 4:12* [f]*Mark 12:44* [g]*Mark 2:11*

THE 153 TEXTS

1. One who wishes to make incense should mix, according to the Law, fragrant resin, cassia, aromatic shell and myrrh in equal amounts.[h] These are the four virtues. With their full and balanced development, the mind will be safe from betrayal.

2. When the soul has been purified through the keeping of all the commandments, it makes the mind steadfast and able to receive the state necessary for prayer.

3. Prayer is communion of the mind with God. What state, then, does the mind need so that it can reach out to its Lord without distraction and commune with him without intermediary?

4. When Moses tried to approach the burning bush, he was forbidden until he had removed his sandals from his feet.[i] If, then, you wish to behold and commune with him who is beyond the perception of the senses and beyond the mind's ability to conceive, you must free yourself from every passionate thought.

[h]Exod. 30:34 [i]Exod. 3:5

5. First pray for the gift of tears, so that through sorrow you may tame that which is savage in your soul. And having confessed your sins to the Lord, you will receive forgiveness from him.

6. Pray with tears, and everything you ask will be heard. For the Lord rejoices greatly when you pray with tears.

7. If you do shed tears during prayer, do not exalt yourself, thinking you are better than others. For your prayer has received help, so that you may confess your sins readily and make peace with the Lord through your tears. Therefore, do not turn the cure for passions into a passion, and so again provoke to anger the one who has given you this grace.

8. Many people, shedding tears for their sins, forget what tears are for, and in their foolishness they go astray.

9. Persevere with patience in your prayer, and send away the concerns and doubts that rise within you. They disturb and trouble you, and by this they weaken the intensity of your prayer.

10. When the demons see you truly eager to pray, they suggest an imaginary need for various things, and then stir up your remembrance of these things, pushing the mind to go after them; and when it fails to find them, it becomes very depressed and miserable. And when the mind is at prayer, the demons keep filling it with the thought of these things, so that it tries to discover more about them and thus loses the fruitfulness of its prayer.

11. Try to make your mind deaf and dumb during prayer; you will then be able to pray.

12. Whenever a temptation or a feeling of contention comes over you, immediately arousing you to anger or to some senseless word, remember your prayer and how you will be judged about it, and at once the disorderly movement within you will subside.

13. Whatever you do to avenge yourself against someone who has wronged you will become a stumbling-block to you during prayer.

14. Prayer is the flower of gentleness and freedom from anger.

15. Prayer is the fruit of joy and thankfulness.

16. Prayer is the cure for gloom and despair.

17. Go and sell all that you have, and give to the poor,[j] and deny yourself, taking up your cross.[k] You will then be free from distraction when you pray.

18. If you desire to pray as you should, deny yourself all the time, and when any kind of affliction troubles you, meditate on prayer.

19. If you endure something painful out of love for wisdom, you will find the fruit of this during prayer.

20. If you desire to pray as you should, do not grieve anyone. Otherwise you run in vain.[l]

21. Leave your gift before the altar. First go away and be reconciled with your brother,[m] and when you return, you will pray undisturbed. For hatred darkens the mind of one who prays, and extinguishes the light of his prayers.

---

[j]Matt. 9:21 [k]Matt. 16:24 [l]Phil. 2:16 [m]Matt. 5:24

22. Those who store up grievances and hatred in themselves are like people who draw water and pour it into a jar full of holes.

23. If you patiently accept what comes, you will always pray with joy.

24. When you pray as you should, thoughts will come to you which make you feel that you have a right to be angry. But anger with your neighbor is never right. If you search, you will find that things can always be arranged without anger. So do all you can to not break out into anger.

25. Take care that, while appearing to cure someone else, you yourself do not remain uncured, in this way thwarting your prayer.

26. If you spare your anger, you yourself will be spared, and you will show your good sense and will be one who prays.

27. If you arm yourself against anger, then you will never succumb to any kind of desire. Desire fuels anger, and anger disturbs spiritual vision, disrupting the state of prayer.

28. Do not pray only with outward forms and gestures, but with reverence and awe try to make your mind conscious of spiritual prayer.

29. Sometimes as soon as you start to pray, you pray well. At other times, in spite of great effort, you do not reach your goal. This is to make you exert yourself even more, so that, having gained the gift of prayer, you keep it safe.

30. When an angel comes to us, all who trouble us withdraw at once. Then the mind is completely calm and prays soundly. But at other times, when the attacks of the demons are particularly strong, the mind does not have a moment of peace. This is because it is weakened by the same passions to which it has succumbed in the past. But if it goes on searching, it will find; and if it knocks, the door will be opened.[n]

31. Do not pray for the fulfillment of your desires, for they may not accord with the will of God. But pray as you have been taught, saying: Your will be done in me.[o] Always pray to

[n]*Matt. 7:8* [o]*Luke 22:42*

him in this way—that his will be done. For he desires what is good and profitable for you, but you do not always ask for this.

32. Often when I have prayed, I have asked for what I thought was good. I persisted in my petition, stupidly begging the will of God, and not leaving it to him to arrange things as he knows is best for me. But when I have received what I asked for, I have been sorry that I did not ask for God's will to be done, because things turned out not to be as I had thought.

33. What is good, except God? Then let us leave everything that concerns us to him, and all will be well. For he who is good is naturally a giver of good gifts.

34. Do not be distressed if you do not immediately receive from God what you ask. He wishes to give you something better, in order to make you persevere in prayer. For what is better than to enjoy God's love and to be in communion with him?

35. Undistracted prayer is the highest function of the mind.

36. Prayer is the ascent of the mind to God.

37. If you desire prayer, renounce everything in order to gain everything.

38. Pray first for the purification of the passions; secondly, for deliverance from ignorance and forgetfulness; and thirdly, for deliverance from all temptation, trial and neglectfulness.

39. In your prayer, seek only righteousness and God's kingdom—that is, virtue and spiritual knowledge. And everything else will be given to you.[p]

40. It is right to pray not only for your own purification, but also for that of all people. By this, you imitate the angels.

41. See whether you stand truly before God in prayer, or are overcome by the desire for human praise, using long prayers as a disguise.

42. Whether you pray with others or alone, try not to pray simply as a routine, but with the conscious awareness of your prayer.

[p] Matt. 6:33

43. Conscious awareness of prayer is concentration joined with reverence, compunction and distress of soul as it confesses its sins with inward sorrow.

44. If your mind is still distracted during prayer, you do not yet know what ascetic prayer is; your prayer is still worldly, embellishing the outer tabernacle.

45. When you pray, keep a close watch on your memory, so that it does not distract you with memories of your past; rather make yourself aware that you are standing before God. For by nature the mind is prone to being carried away by memories during prayer.

46. While you are praying, the memory brings before you fantasies of the past, or of recent concerns, or of the face of someone who has irritated you.

47. The demon is very envious of us when we pray, and uses every kind of trick to interfere with our intention. So he is always using our memory to stir up thoughts, and our flesh to arouse the passions, in order to obstruct our way of ascending to God.

48. When the demon fails, after many attempts, to hinder the prayer of the righteous, he slackens his efforts a little. The demon then succeeds later when the person has finished praying, either by provoking him to anger, destroying the prayer's good effects, or else by exciting him to senseless pleasure, degrading his mind.

49. When you have prayed as you should, expect the demon to attack you. Stand on guard, ready to protect the fruits of your prayer. From the start, this is your task: to cultivate and to protect.[q] Therefore, having cultivated, do not leave the fruits unprotected; otherwise you will gain nothing from your prayer.

50. The warfare between us and the demons is waged exclusively on account of spiritual prayer. For prayer is detestable and offensive to them, while it leads us to salvation and peace.

51. What do the demons desire to excite within us? Gluttony, lust, greed, anger, hate, and the rest of the passions, so that the mind grows

---

[q] *Gen. 2:15*

coarse and cannot pray as it should. For when the passions are aroused in the irrational part of our nature, they do not allow the mind to function properly.

52. We practice the virtues in order to achieve contemplation of the inner essences[r] of created things, and from this we pass to contemplation of the Word who gives them their being; and he manifests himself when we are in the state of prayer.

53. The state of prayer is dispassionate, which by virtue of the most intense love transports the mind to the noetic realm that it longs for.

54. One who desires to pray truly must not only control his tendency to be provoked and his desire, but he must also free himself from every passionate thought.

55. One who loves God is always communing with him as his Father, pushing away every passionate thought.

56. To achieve dispassion is not necessarily to achieve pure prayer. One may still be occupied

---

[r] *Logoi*

with thoughts, which may be dispassionate, but still distract him and keep him far from God.

57. When the mind is no longer amused with dispassionate thoughts about various things, it has not necessarily reached the realm of prayer, for it may still be contemplating the inner essences of these things. Although this contemplation is dispassionate, it is still concerned with created things, so it fills the mind with their forms and keeps it away from God.

58. If the mind has not risen above the contemplation of the created world, it has not yet seen the realm of God perfectly. For it may be occupied with the knowledge of knowable things, and so involved in how many such things there are.

59. If you desire to pray, you need God, who gives prayer to the one who prays.[s] Invoke him, then, saying: May your Name be hallowed, your kingdom come[t]—that is, the Holy Spirit and your only-begotten Son. For this is what he taught us, saying: Worship the Father in spirit and in truth.[u]

[s]*I Sam. 2:9* LXX [t]*Matt. 6:9-10* [u]*John 4:24*

60. One who prays in spirit and in truth is no longer dependent on created things when honoring the Creator, but praises him for and in himself.

61. If you are a theologian, you will pray truly. And if you pray truly, you are a theologian.

62. When your intellect, in its great longing for God, gradually withdraws from the flesh and turns away from all thoughts that have their source in your senses, memory, or soul–body temperament, and when it becomes full of reverence and joy, then you may conclude that you are close to the frontiers of prayer.

63. The Holy Spirit, out of compassion for our weakness, comes to us even when we are impure. And if only he finds our mind truly praying to him, he enters it and drives out all the many thoughts and ideas swarming within it, and he arouses in it a longing for spiritual prayer.

64. While everything else produces thoughts and ideas and speculations in the mind through changes in the body, the Lord does the opposite, by entering the mind. He fills it with whatever knowledge he desires, and through the mind he calms the body's uncontrolled impulses.

65. One who loves true prayer, and yet becomes angry or resentful, is his own enemy. It is as if he damages his own eyes in order to see more clearly.

66. If you deeply desire prayer, do nothing that is opposed to prayer, so that God may come near and be with you.

67. When you are praying, do not form within yourself an image of the Deity, and do not let your mind be stamped with the impression of any form. Rather, approach the Immaterial in an immaterial manner, and then you will understand.

68. Be on your guard against the tricks of the demons. When you are praying purely and calmly, sometimes they suddenly bring before you a strange and alien form, making you imagine in your pride that the Deity is there. They are trying to convince you that what was shown you is the Deity, but in truth the Deity has no quantity or form.

69. When the jealous demon fails to stir up our memory during prayer, he disturbs the soul–body temperament, so as to conjure up some strange fantasy in the mind. Since your mind is usually preoccupied with thoughts, it is easily distracted. Rather than pursuing immaterial and formless knowledge, it is deceived mistaking smoke for light.

70. Stand on guard and protect your mind from thoughts while you pray. Then your mind will complete its prayer and continue in its natural tranquility. In this way, the One who has compassion on the ignorant will come to you, and you will receive the blessed gift of prayer.

71. You cannot achieve pure prayer while you are entangled in material things and troubled by constant concerns. Prayer means the shedding of thoughts.

72. One who is bound up cannot run; nor can the mind that is enslaved to passion perceive the realm of spiritual prayer. For it is dragged about by passionate thoughts and cannot stay still.

73. When the mind achieves prayer that is pure and free from passion, the demons no longer attack with evil thoughts, but with thoughts of what is good. For they suggest to the mind an illusion of God's glory in a pleasing form, making it think it has reached the final goal of prayer. A certain man who has spiritual knowledge has said that this illusion results from the passion of self-esteem and from the demon's touch on a certain area of the brain.

74. I think that the demon, by touching this area, changes the light surrounding the mind as he likes. In this way, he uses the passion of self-esteem to stir up a thought in the mind that stupidly attributes form and location to divine and principal knowledge. Not being disturbed by impure and carnal passions, but thinking itself to be pure, the mind imagines that there is no longer any adverse energy within it. It then mistakes the appearance produced by the demon for a divine manifestation, though it is the demon who cunningly manipulates the brain, as we have described.

75. When the angel of God comes to us, with his presence alone he puts an end to all adverse energy within the mind and makes its light energize without illusion.

76. The statement in the Apocalypse that an angel brought incense and offered it with the prayers of the saints[v] refers, I think, to this grace when it is energized through the angel. For it instills knowledge of true prayer, so that the mind stands firm, free from all agitation, lethargy and negligence.

77. The bowls of incense which the twenty-four elders offered are said to be the prayers of the saints. The bowls should be understood as friendship with God or perfect spiritual love, by which prayer is energized in spirit and in truth.

78. When you think that you do not need to shed tears for your sins during prayer, reflect on this: you should always be in God, but you are still far away from him. Then you will weep with greater feeling.

---

[v]*Rev. 8:3*

79. When you do realize where you are, you will certainly and gladly sorrow, and like Isaiah, you will rebuke yourself. For, being unclean, dwelling in the midst of an unclean people—that is, your enemies—you dare to stand before the Lord of Hosts.[w]

80. If you pray truly, you will gain great assurance. Angels will come to you as they came to Daniel, and they will enlighten you with the knowledge of the inner essence of created things.[x]

81. Know that the holy angels encourage us to pray and stand beside us, rejoicing and praying with us.[y] Therefore, if we are negligent and allow thoughts from the enemy into our mind, we greatly provoke the angels. For while they struggle hard on our behalf, we do not even take the trouble to pray to God for ourselves. We despise their services to us, and abandoning their Lord and God, we partner with unclean demons.

82. Pray gently and calmly, sing with understanding and rhythm; then you will soar like an eagle high in the heavens.

---

[w]*Isa. 6:5* [x]*Dan. 2:19* [y]*Tobit 12:12*

83. Psalmody calms the passions and curbs the uncontrolled impulses of the body, and prayer enables the mind to activate its own energy.

84. Prayer is the energy which accords with the dignity of the mind. It is the mind's true and highest activity.

85. Psalmody belongs to the wisdom of the world of multiplicity; prayer is the prelude to the immaterial knowledge of the One.

86. Spiritual knowledge has great beauty. It is the helpmate of prayer, awakening the noetic power of the mind to contemplate divine knowledge.

87. If you have not yet received the gift of prayer or psalmody, persevere patiently and you will receive it.

88. "He spoke a parable to them to this end, that men ought always to pray, and not lose heart."[z] So do not lose heart and despair because you have not yet received the gift of prayer. You will receive it later. In the same parable we read: "Though I do not fear God, or man's

---

[z] *Luke 18:1*

opinion, yet because the widow troubles me, I will vindicate her." In the same way, God will quickly vindicate those who cry to him day and night. Take heart, then, and persevere diligently in holy prayer.

89. You should desire for your affairs to work out not as you think best, but according to God's will. Then you will be undisturbed and thankful in your prayer.

90. Even if you think you are with God, be on your guard against the demon of lust. For he is very crafty and jealous. He tries to outwit the activity and watchfulness of your mind and draw it away from God, when it stands before him with reverence and fear.

91. If you cultivate prayer, be ready for demonic attacks and endure them with resolve. They will come at you like wild beasts and attack your whole body.

92. Prepare yourself like an experienced fighter. Even if you see a sudden apparition, do not be shaken. If you see a sword drawn against you, or a torch thrust in your face, do not be alarmed. If you see a revolting and bloody figure, do not panic. Stand fast, boldly affirming your faith, and you will be more resolute in confronting your enemies.

93. One who bears distress patiently will achieve joy, and one who endures the repulsive will know delight.

94. Take care that you are not deceived by some vision shown you by the crafty demons. Be on your guard, turn to prayer and ask God to show you if it comes from him. And if it does not, scatter the illusion at once. Do not be afraid, for if you pray fervently to God, the demons will retreat, being lashed by his unseen power.

95. You should be aware of this trick: sometimes the demons will split into two groups, and when you call for help against one group, the other will come, disguised as angels, and drive away the first. By this, they deceive you into believing that they are truly angels.

96. Cultivate great humility and courage, and you will escape the power of the demons. "No plague shall come near your dwelling, for he shall give his angels charge over you."[a] And they will invisibly repel all the energy of the enemy.

97. One who practices pure prayer will hear the demons crashing and banging, shouting and cursing. But he will not be overwhelmed or lose his mind; he will say to God: "I will fear no evil, for you are with me,"[b] and other words of this kind.

98. At the time of such trials, use a brief but intense prayer.

99. If the demons suddenly threaten to appear out of the air, to frighten you and take possession of your mind, do not be frightened and pay no attention to their threats. For they are trying to terrify you, to see whether you take notice of them or scorn them completely.

100. When you stand in prayer before Almighty God, who created all things and takes thought

---

[a]Ps. 90/91:10-11 [b]Ps. 22/23:4

for all, why are you so foolish as to forget the fear of God, and be afraid of mosquitoes and cockroaches? Have you not heard it said: "You shall fear the Lord your God,"*c* and, "Fear and dread shall fall upon them"?*d*

101. Bread is food for the body, holiness is food for the soul, and spiritual prayer is food for the mind.

102. When you are in the inner temple, do not pray like the Pharisee, but like the Publican, that you may also be set free by the Lord.*e*

103. Try not to pray against someone, lest you destroy what you are building and make your prayer loathsome.

104. Learn from the man who owed ten thousand talents: if you do not forgive your debtor, you yourself will not be forgiven. For it is said: "He delivered him to the tormentors."*f*

105. Detach yourself from bodily concerns when you pray. Do not let the bite of a flea or fly, or the sting of a louse or a mosquito, deprive you of the fruits of your prayer.

---

*c**Deut. 6:13* *d**Exod. 15:16* *e**Luke 18:10-14* *f**Matt. 18:34*

106. We have heard that the evil one attacked a certain saint so fiercely as he prayed that, when the saint lifted his hands, the evil one changed himself into a lion. Raising his front legs, he fixed his claws into the saint's thighs, keeping them there until the saint lowered his hands—which was only when he had reached the end of his usual prayers.

107. There is also the case of a great monk, John the Small. He lived the life of contemplative prayer in a pit, and his communion with God was not interrupted even when a demon in the form of a serpent wrapped itself around him, chewed his flesh and spat it out into his face.

108. You have surely read the lives of the monks of Tabennesis. When Abba Theodore was preaching to the brethren, two vipers crawled under his feet, but he calmly made an arch with his feet and let them stay there until he had finished his sermon. Then he showed the vipers to the brethren and told them what had happened.

109. We read how, when another spiritual brother was praying, a viper came and wrapped itself around his leg. But he did not lower his hands until he had finished all his usual prayers. Because he loved God more than himself, he was not harmed at all.

110. Do not let your eyes be distracted during prayer, but detach yourself from concerns over body and soul, and give all your attention to the mind.

111. Another saint living the life of contemplative prayer in the desert was attacked during prayer by demons, who for two weeks tossed him in the air like a ball, catching him in his mat. They utterly failed to distract his mind from fiery prayer.

112. When another monk was practicing prayer as he journeyed in the desert, two angels came and walked on either side of him. But he paid them no heed, for he did not wish to lose what was better. He remembered the Apostle's words: "Neither angels, nor principalities, nor powers ... shall be able to separate us from the love of Christ."[g]

[g] *Rom. 8:38-39*

113. One becomes equal to the angels through prayer, for he longs to "behold the face of the Father who is in heaven."[h]

114. Never try to see a form or image during prayer.

115. Do not desire to have a sensory image of angels or powers or Christ, for this would be madness. It would be to take a wolf as your shepherd and to worship your enemies, the demons.

116. Self-esteem is the start of illusions in the mind. Under its impulse, the mind tries to enclose the Deity in shapes and images.

117. I say again what I have said before: blessed is the mind that is completely free from images during prayer.

118. Blessed is the mind that is undistracted in prayer and acquires an ever greater longing for God.

119. Blessed is the mind that is free from the material during prayer and is stripped of all possessions.

120. Blessed is the mind that has acquired complete freedom from sensations during prayer.

---

[h]*Matt. 18:10*

121. Blessed is the one who regards every person as god after God.

122. Blessed is the one who looks joyfully on the salvation and progress of everyone as if they were his own.

123. Blessed is the one who regards himself as "the off-scouring of all things."[i]

124. A monk is one who is separated from all and united with all.

125. A monk is one who considers himself as linked with every other person, by seeing himself in each one.

126. One who always dedicates his first thoughts to God has perfect prayer.

127. If you want to pray as a monk, shun all lies and take no oath. Otherwise you vainly pretend to be what you are not.

128. If you desire to pray in spirit, be detached from the flesh, and no cloud will darken you during prayer.

---

[i] *I Cor. 4:13*

129. Entrust the needs of your body to God, and it will be clear that you entrust the needs of your spirit to him also.

130. If you receive what has been promised, you will reign over all things. And keeping these promises in mind, you will gladly endure your present poverty, spiritual and material.

131. Do not shun poverty and affliction: the fuel that gives wings to prayer.

132. Let the virtues of the body lead you to those of the soul; and the virtues of the soul to those of the spirit; and these, in turn, to immaterial and principal knowledge.

133. If you are praying to overcome some thought, and it subsides easily, discern carefully how this took place. Otherwise, you may be deluded into attributing the cause to yourself.

134. There are times when the demons suggest thoughts to you and then urge you to fight against them with prayer; after this, they withdraw on their own, deceiving you into imagining you have begun to overcome such thoughts and to drive away the demons.

135. If you pray to overcome a passion or demon who is troubling you, remember the words: "I will pursue my enemies and overtake them; and I will not turn back until they are consumed. I will dash them to pieces and they shall not be able to stand: they shall fall under my feet."[j] Say this whenever necessary, and by this, arm yourself with humility against your enemies.

136. Do not think that you have acquired holiness unless you have reached the point of shedding blood to attain it. For, according to the Apostle, we must battle relentlessly against sin, even if it means death.[k]

137. If you do good to one person, you may be wronged by another, and so feel injured, and say or do something stupid. By this, you squander what you gained with your good deed by your bad deed. This is exactly what the demons want, so always pay attention.

138. Be ready for the attacks of the demons, and think how to avoid becoming their slave.

---

[j]*Ps. 17/18:37-38* LXX [k]*Eph. 6:11-17; Heb. 12:4*

139. At night, the cunning demons try to disturb the spiritual teacher by direct attack. In the daytime, they attack him through other people, besieging him with slander, distractions and danger.

140. Do not try to avoid the fullers.[l] Let them beat, trample, stretch and smooth, and your garments will be all the brighter.

141. Until you renounce the passions, your mind will be opposed to holiness and truth. You will not find the fragrance of incense in your breast.

142. Do you have a longing for prayer? Then leave the things of this world and live your life in heaven—not just in theory, but through angelic action and divine knowledge.

143. If you only remember the Judge, how awesome and impartial he is, in times of adversity, you have not yet learned to serve the Lord with fear and rejoice in him with trembling.[m] For, even in a state of spiritual peace and blessedness you should still worship him with reverence and awe.

---

[l] *A fuller is one who cleans and shrinks fabric using heat and pressure; an image of the demons: resisting their temptations leads to our purification.* [m] *Ps. 2:1*

144. Until one is completely changed by repentance, he would be wise to always remember his sins with sorrow and recall the eternal fire which they justly deserve.

145. If one shamelessly dares to reach out for divine knowledge, or even embark upon immaterial prayer, while he is still wrapped up in sinfulness and anger, he deserves the apostolic rebuke; for it is dangerous for him to pray with his head bare and uncovered. Such a soul, he says, ought to be veiled because of the angels who are present,[n] and be clothed in due reverence and humility.

146. Just as staring into the noonday sun will not cure an ailment of the eyes, so also the counterfeit practice of fearful and heavenly prayer—which ought to be performed in spirit and in truth—will in no way benefit a mind that is passionate and impure. On the contrary, such practice will provoke the wrath of God against that mind.

147. If the One who needs nothing and shows no favors did not receive the one who came to

---

[n] *I Cor. 11:5-7*

the altar without being reconciled with his neighbor who had something against him,[o] consider how much we must be on guard and discern if we should offer at the spiritual altar incense that is acceptable to God.

148. Do not delight in words of glory. Otherwise the demons will no longer work behind your back, but openly before your face. They will laugh and mock you during prayer, drawing you away and enticing you into alien thoughts.

149. If you seek prayer attentively, you will find it; for nothing is more essential to prayer than attentiveness. So do all you can to acquire it.

150. As sight is superior to all the other senses, so prayer is more divine than all the other virtues.

151. The value of prayer lies not in mere quantity, but in its quality. This is shown by the contrast of the two men who went up into the temple,[p] and by the command: "When you pray, do not use vain repetitions."[q]

---

[o]Matt. 5:23-24 [p]Luke 18:10 [q]Matt. 6:7

152. So long as you give attention to the beauty of the body, and you give thought to delights outside of the tabernacle, you have not yet perceived the reality of prayer, and are still far from walking its blessed path.

153. If, when you pray, no other joy can attract you, then truly you have found prayer. ✠

Continue your exploration of the history and worship of historical Christianity with fine titles and more from

Legacy Icons
www.legacyicons.com

Saint Ignatius Orthodox Press
www.ignatius.cc